TRIBE OF ARBITRAGERS

SHORT ARBITRAGE ADVICE FROM
SUCCESSFUL ONLINE RESELLERS

KEV BLACKBURN

LEGAL NOTICE & DISCLAIMER

Copyright: Life Success Engineer**.**

Published By: Kev Blackburn.

Publication Date: 22nd September 2019.

Edition: 1

Website: https://www.lifesuccessengineer.com

Email: support@lifesuccessengineer.com

Affiliate Links. This book may contain affiliate links. If you purchase a product through one of them, I will receive a commission (at no additional cost to you). I only ever endorse products that I have personally used and benefitted from personally. Thank you for all your support.

PRAISE FOR TRIBE OF ARBITRAGERS

Throughout the creation of the Tribe Of Arbitragers Project, we have many community and mastermind members that have expressed the following comments, opinions, reviews and feedback on the content shared within this book, which has been amazing to see, read, and experience.

This book has been made by Amazon Sellers as a gift to all other Amazon Sellers.

Just some of the comments are below:

"This is the perfect resource for you to learn what has worked for others and what has not worked for others while allowing you to expand your mastermind and network making relationships with others on the same path as you"

"A thousand thanks for this Kev and Jake! Truly valuable once again!"

"These videos are priceless! Thanks, Kev and Dev!"

"Great chat. Biggest takeaway - Anything is possible!"

"Thanks Kev, Another insightful brilliant video. Keep up the great work!"

"Thank you guys, so much wisdom in what he's saying. Great!"

"Never chase the money it's time that's finite."

"Kev and Andy, great session!"

"Excellent interview and super advice from Reezy"

"Discipline is the hardest and most integral part of it all. Well done guys ;)"

"Inspiring stuff guys. Love the interview "

"What Kev has achieved here is amazing?!"

"Thanks David and Kev. The last answer resonated"

"Great energy and episode!"

"Inspiring Stuff Guys"

"Some great nuggets of ideas to take out from this excellent interview"

"What an incredible video, always loving these interviews"

"I'm so excited!"

"It's amazing to see so many amazing people together in one place"

ACKNOWLEDGEMENTS

As I begin to reflect on the Tribe Of Arbitragers Project, I would like to take the opportunity to thank all the amazing people that have contributed to the creation of this book.

Firstly, to my family, Kylie, Theo & Harper for the support they give every day. Everything I do is for them and everything we have done has been together. Your love and support is my ultimate strength.

To the tribe members featured throughout the book who have taken the time out of their day to share real stories of success and failure without holding anything back. Your generosity to share with others is a gift that makes our community truly special. Thank you all, I'm grateful for your honesty, participation and your super valued time.

One of the core values I wanted to instil within the project is to have real people sharing real stories and experiences that can help, support, motivate and inspire others to take massive action. True references of success can be the trigger for others to believe they can do it too.

To our entire team that continues to work relentlessly with energy and passion every day to fulfill our mission to inspire millions of people that each of us has the potential to build lives to any level of success we desire. Create the vision and then have the courage to take massive focused action to achieve your goals and dreams.

To my mastermind, Gareth, Izaak & Brandon that have walked the walk side by side since day one. Believing we can all win together remains our greatest common drive.

To the Life Success Engineer community and mastermind members that have liked commented or shared any content, I have ever created. Your encouragement, support and feedback have given me the confidence to believe in myself. I'm incredibly thankful for everyone and looking forward to continuing to build and serve you for years to come. Bring it on #TeamMassiveAction.

And finally, I would like to take this moment to thank you for being here and reading this book. This is a personal message from me to you to say you can do this. Whatever situation you find yourself in, always remember that one piece of information or advice can change your entire life. The only responsibility you have is to take massive action on it. The road ahead will be long but with the grit, tenacity, and desire, nothing can ever stop you.

To all of our continued massive success together,

Kev "Massive Action" Blackburn

LIFESUCCESSENGINEER

OUR 'TRIBE OF ARBITRAGERS' MISSION

The Tribe Of Arbitragers mission is to give you short and actionable advice that you can apply into your life and business. It will connect you with people that have taken action and began the journey to building life on their terms. It will expand your network and your mastermind peers. Whether you are interested in Wholesale, Online Arbitrage, Retail Arbitrage or Books, there are people here that would welcome you by sharing real stories and real experiences. To achieve this mission, I set out on this project to ask everyone 6 powerful questions. This book is not designed to be a step-by-step training guide on how to get started and build your business. Resources and recommendations will be listed at the end of the book for this.

THE 6 POWER QUESTIONS

These 6 power questions have been asked of people that have built businesses ranging from part-time sellers to full time multiple 6, 7 or even 8 figures:

1. How has a failure or apparent failure, set you up for later success? Do you have a "favourite failure" of yours?

2. What is one of the best or most worthwhile investments you've ever made? (Could be time, money, energy, etc.)

3. In the last 5 years, what new belief, behaviour, or habit has most improved your life?

4. What best advice would you give to someone about to enter the world of arbitrage?

5. What are the bad recommendations you hear relating to arbitrage?

6. When you feel overwhelmed or unfocused, or have lost your focus temporarily what do you do?

CONTENTS

INTRODUCTION

Dear Friend,

In June 2015, I discovered an amazing opportunity that we all have available today called Amazon FBA. For decades, normal people like you and I would have to work tirelessly to try building a physical product business from home or brick and mortar stores.

Jeff Bezos and Amazon changed the landscape forever when they created what we now know and leverage called Amazon FBA, Fulfilment By Amazon. This gives us the ability to reach millions of customers worldwide while using the infrastructure they have to ship orders to customers 24 hours a day, 365 days a year.

Since we began our journey, we have sold multiple 7 figures, quit our jobs, moved into a warehouse and now we have a full-time team working for us every day. This book is a tool for you to learn from many sellers within our mastermind that are on the same path. If you are interested in my full story, I've added my full story at the end for you.

From this point forward, there will be many tips, guidance notes, and resources that will support your journey from where you are today at any level you want to be. Use it. Take massive action on it. We are here to support you so after every interview, there are links to the person for you to reach out to if you want.

I want to show you what can be achieved. I want to inspire you to take massive action to find out what you can achieve. I know you can do it.

Finally, if you like the book and receive value from it, would you please review a review on Amazon to share your thoughts on it. We would appreciate you for it.

To your massive success,

Kev "Massive Action" Blackburn

LIFESUCCESSENGINEER

Life Success Engineer:
https://www.lifesuccessengineer.com/

Massive Action Academy:
https://www.lifesuccessengineer.com/academy

YouTube Channel:

http://lifesuccessengineer.com/youtube

Instagram Page:
http://lifesuccessengineer.com/instagram

THE AMAZON FBA BUSINESS MODELS

We are living in the greatest age today to build an eCommerce business using Amazon FBA. We can leverage Amazon's $240 BILLION global operations to reach millions of Amazon's customers that now have two decades worth of trust and loyalty that buy throughout the year on the Amazon Marketplace.

For those interested in building a business, it's the perfect opportunity that gives you the potential to build multiple million pound or dollar businesses. In today's world, it has now become a question of desire, drive, tenacity, and determination. The opportunity is there.

Here are the business models you can build depending on your available resources and after every tribe members answer, you will see which businesses model you can follow them on and learn more about.

1. Online Arbitrage
2. Retail Arbitrage
3. Wholesale
4. Books

YOUR BUSINESS OBJECTIVE

Start with the end in mind. Why are you building this business in the first place? This business can consume every hour of the day and accept it takes hard work for a long time. Therefore I want to ask you if you know your business objective is, take some time to get clear on your goal which can keep you reminded and focused on building your business in the right way from the beginning.

Here is how I set up an annual year building my Amazon business freedom focused:

Q1 – Planting Seeds

January, February & March are months to take big bold actions in your business. These are strategically planned risks you can take in your business that can have a huge upside later in the year.

Q2 – Training & Development

April, May & June are focused around training and developing the seeds you have planted. Take your time here and go deep into the process. The leverage here is perfect.

Q3 – Streamlining & Efficiency

July, August & September are the months to cut the fat. Where can you save time? Where can you optimise your processes? Are your processes still relevant or redundant?

Q4 – Maximising Profit & Minimising Time

October, November & December are now the months for you to reap rewards on the massive action you have taken!

TRIBE MEMBER 1: KEV BLACKBURN

I'm Kev Blackburn, business systemisation and automation specialist, massive action success coach, philanthropist, founder of Life Success Engineer and author of best selling book Tribe Of Arbitragers.

Graduating from university in 2014 with a first-class degree in Electrical Engineering, I suddenly realised that there was more to life than what I had built myself. I had a young family and all I wanted to do is support them but the trouble was, I had built a life without freedom or control to be with them.

In 2015, I had the opportunity of a lifetime when I came across Amazon FBA and the online business model Online Arbitrage. We went all in and we were able to quit our jobs and move into a warehouse within 12 months. We are now on the road to £10,000,000 in sales.

In 2016, I began getting more and more involved in Personal Development and challenging myself to become better every day in all areas of my life. This allowed me to become aware of areas of life that I had neglected and was suffering in.

I launched Life Success Engineer as a vehicle for me to share my journey and in the process support as many people as possible contributing to others as much as possible. I share everything I possibly can from mindset, beliefs, strategies, online business, productivity, goal setting, motivation and much more with a very simple mission, inspire massive action! It's been an incredible journey up until this point and it's given me the amazing gift of meeting so many inspiring people.

People have asked me to share a deeper look into my story so I thought I would take this opportunity now before I answer the questions. Word of warning, I'm going to go a little deep and not hold back so take a deep breath, here goes...

I was born in Frankfurt, Germany, on 22nd October 1988 to my German mother and my American father. Unfortunately, as I was born, my father who a soldier in the US army had to leave which left my mother to take care of us alone and since that time I have never had my father around. When I was 5 years old my mother met an English man to whom my little brother was born and we moved to England in 1993/94. It was a complicated start to life but you cannot choose who you are or what cards you are dealt with. You have to use it to your advantage and fuel your strength. England is all I have ever known as I was integrated into school easily and learned the language fast. Everything was great until I was 11 years old when my mother became incredibly unwell and was forced to move back to Germany leaving us all behind. I remember the time like it was yesterday and the experience is the foundation of who I am today. I came home from school one afternoon and she had disappeared. This was a devastating, worrying and confusing time for my family. A decision was made by my sister to take me in and look after me, which ended up being the turning point in my life. This saved me from going into care. I'm forever grateful for her. I want to stress and highlight I do not blame my mother for this time. She is the reason I am the person I am today. When a parent becomes so ill they feel no way out other than to leave their children, an incredible amount of care and support for that person is needed. I swore to myself at 11 I would never be any trouble to my family and I would become the best person I could so that one day I can provide for my own family. Fast forward nearly 2 decades and I have an amazing and caring relationship with my mother plus recently I had the most beautiful gift of giving my sister away at her wedding day.

Being unaware of what I wanted to do in my life, all I knew I enjoyed maths, science, and electronics. The obvious choice for me was Electrical Engineering. I got fantastic results at GCSE and very proud of the achievements I made during this time when things could have been so different. Adulthood seemed to come around so quickly as I turned up at college seemly being funneled down the education route. A decision was made after 1 year at 6th form college that I would quit and join an apprenticeship. This was one of the best decisions I made as it gave me the hands-on skills that were required while still studying for my degree. At this point, I thought this is what I wanted as a trade would be a well-paid career to support my future family.

As we all know, life isn't so straightforward.

Meeting Kylie during a walk home from a part-time job I had during the first year of the course, my life would never be the same again. Driving past in her car, she had become friends with some of my old school friends so they stopped. After reconnecting, we started to hang out and it was on Kylie's 18th birthday we entered a relationship. We got the news that most 18 years would fear the most that we were going to become parents at the fresh age of 19. Although it was a shock, Kylie and I have never looked back and we were blessed with our son, Theo. This gave me more drive and desire to provide for them and become that Engineer would support our family.

I successfully went through the apprenticeship providing for our young family finally becoming a qualified electrical tradesman. I honestly believed our life's direction was going exactly as planned. Every year as we grew would become easier. I would get a pay rise and things would be ok. I lived believing this story up until I made it to an Electrical Engineer.

At this point, something magical happened...

Our 2nd child in January 2015, Harper, blessed us and our beautiful family was complete. Life had become exactly as we envisioned but something was missing because it didn't feel right. It suddenly dawned on me that this pattern of life is like so many others. Living a tradition life and trying our best to make ends meet. As our wages grew, so did our expenses. I realised nobody throughout my entire education taught me about money and how to manage it. Somehow we just were going from month to month waiting to be paid again. This was the moment I was "plugged out the matrix", I snapped and I told myself I will not live like this anymore! I was now seeking an opportunity to do something extraordinary in life. The goal was now to be with my family every day and for as long as I want. I wanted to have total freedom in life. This is what truly made me feel fulfilled and happy. Not the significance of the job title. That is when I get the chance to start an Online Business with Amazon FBA. We began selling on Amazon in June 2015 and scaled our sales up to £150,000 in 6 months so we just went all in and quit our jobs. We began this from our living room while I was still working and Kylie was on maternity with Harper. It wasn't easy and huge sacrifices were made to make it work but we made it to the point where we could work for ourselves. Kylie would be in charge of the shipping while I was in charge of the virtual side of the operations. I would source products every day and would challenge myself to hit purchasing targets daily. I did whatever I had to do, wake up early and go to bed late. During dinner times, I no longer read the newspapers and instead I drove home to pick on the day's shipment boxes to take to the UPS drop off point. This was the entire repetitive system for 6 months. Wake up, source products, recruit and train assistants, review products, purchase products, take shipments to UPS drop off point and get home later after work to source more. Blood, sweat and massive action tears every single day.

Our mission was to get out of our home and into a warehouse. The house became too much for us to separate personal life to professional life so we were super focused all in to get to this point. We made it in June 2016 when we walked into our brand new warehouse that was incredibly significant for us at the time. It gave us the belief that we could continue to build the business to the goals we have. During this time, we had built a bigger team both at the warehouse and virtually online. We had our first warehouse processor in Amber and we also had a full virtual assistant team that supported us to source products every day and purchase products everyday. I had become the purchaser in the business as at that time we had Kylie & Amber managing shipments while Hari (first senior assistant) had become my reviewer and sourcing team leader. Purchasing was the final stage to outsource that would give us the potential to be out of operations while operations continued. It took me around 3 months to build the confidence to outsource purchasing but to be honest, it should have been done much sooner. Such much of business is your mindset and your comfort zone. My best advice now is to anyone, what is honestly the worst thing that can happen and is it as bad as you think in reality?

This is what gave us the first experiences of freedom in life having a business that would run and be managed 100% without Kylie and me to manage operations. It is what started to plant the seed of wanting to help and support other people by simply asking the question, how do you want to live life? If we had not asked this and came to become aware that all we wanted to do is live life on our terms to enjoy time with loved ones and friends, we would never have been open to this opportunity.

During this time, I invested heavily in my personal development spending £1000's on coaches, training programs and seminars. Being introduced to Personal Development was a defining part of this journey. I will never forget the first 22 minutes I listened to from Jim Rohn. It was that powerful it changed my entire belief system that we are in control of our lives. Since then I have learned so much from so many of my mentors from Tony Robbins, Les Brown, Eric Thomas, Gary Vee, Grant Cardone and also Stefan James. Becoming self-aware of why I do what I do and how I can change it to create success in life is the most powerful transformation anyone can make in life. This was the birth of Life Success Engineer because I just wanted to share and inspire massive action to achieve whatever goals you have in life.

In 2017 we experienced first hand the need to build multiple streams of income. While we were in a position of great times in the business, it all came crashing around us when our account was suspended due to an unforeseen ingredient we were not allowed to sell. This hit us hard taking our sales from £2000 - £4000 a day to £0 overnight. This made us realise the importance of building systems that would allow us to scale while starting other businesses.

Many lessons were learned at this time and the importance of team building cannot be underestimated. Nothing would be possible without a team and we have an incredible group of people that now build this business with us. This has allowed us as a family to experience magic moments that have been truly magical for us seeing parts of the world that were literally on our bucket list when we began this journey, which makes everything worth it. I'm so thankful that I was blessed with Kylie and that we had the courage to come together and build our lives together.

This is why I do not just solely talk and share things about business or just personal development. They do go hand in hand together because as you grow, everything around you will too. That is the mission behind the Massive Action Movement.

Let's get to the questions…

How has a failure or apparent failure, set you up for later success? Do you have a "favourite failure" of yours?

Since 2015 I think I have failed every day going into the unknown starting an Online Business. I realized on day 1 that taking massive action is the ONLY way of making any progress. Progress comes in many forms: success, failure, confusion, frustration, discipline, consistency and much more. Every time you take action, you will always get some sort of feedback, which is always useful. Becoming comfortable with failure is the key to long-term success because the path to success is all about how much discomfort you can handle.

I would say my "favourite failure" was moving into our warehouse without honestly knowing whether we were ready for it or even afford it. We see it now as a massive success but at the time, the unawareness and confusion taught me to be bold and step up to taking massive action. Go all in! Walking into a 2000 square foot warehouse, we started working on the floor with no furniture and every day we were committed to taking another step forward. It created a vacuum effect where it immediately gave us a sense of "we haven't achieved" anything yet and we must fill this space as soon as possible.

What is one of the best or most worthwhile investments you've ever made? (Could be time, money, energy, etc.)

What a great question? I've made so many investments now that I can honestly say that EVERY investment in my personal development and growth has had huge returns in either business growth, freedom of time, working more efficiently or a change in belief.

The first investment I'd highlight is that I purchased a book for £2.99 called "The Strangest Secret" by Earl Nightingale. This planted the seed to wonder what is the difference between those that become successful long term and those that do not. It started making me look at myself and ask important questions. Amazing book.

The second investment has to be Tony Robbins Unleash The Power Within. Having attended twice as a participant and then the third as a crewmember, this seminar didn't just give me a definition of energy; it SHOWED me the definition of energy! The energy required achieving ANY goal despite how hard it may seem.

In the last 5 years, what new belief, behaviour, or habit has most improved your life?

I'd dedicate this question to the great late Jim Rohn. I learned so many life-changing fundamentals that changed my core identity. He literally changed how I viewed the world. Just some of them are below:

"Work harder on yourself than you do on your job"

"It's not what happens, it what you do"

"Failure is a few errors in judgment repeated every day"

"Success is a few simple disciplines practiced every day"

The power of these seeds allows me every day to be the best I can be and take action in what I believe to be correct. Along with "Life is always happening for us, not to us" and "if you want to take on the island, burn your f**King boats".

What best advice would you give to someone about to enter the world of arbitrage?

Watch my "10 Hard Truths Why People Fail With Online Arbitrage " video and "Online Arbitrage For Beginners" playlist. These will give you a solid understanding of how to start, get your first sales and build a business. Shared at the end of this book.

What are bad recommendations you hear relating to arbitrage?

Difficult question to answer as there are many cases of "bad recommendations".

If I had to give you a real example right now I would say when people give a "guideline" for best sales rank. A common one is "make sure it's 100,000 sales rank or less in Toys & Games". I always say to anyone that you MUST look at the real-time data over the last 1, 3, 6 months. What has that product been doing? You NEVER want to make a purchasing decision based on a single moment in time.

When you feel overwhelmed or unfocused, or have lost your focus temporarily what do you do?

Whenever I feel this way it is usually down to lack of preparation. Planning and being organized is SUPER important when it comes to productivity in my life. If I do not plan or have goals in mind that I would like to achieve, it's very easy to get lost and not know what you are doing. Some amazing books like the "The One Thing" and "Deep work" really try to help with this.

You will discover that we can only work "deeply" for a period of 45 to 90 minutes. This is when we have a clear outcome that we were looking to achieve. I try to work in these time blocks so that I can be at my best in terms of focus and energy.

Taking your mind from work also helps so I often do exercise or spend some time being unplugged in a hobby such as watching movies for example.

Video Link: https://youtu.be/GlvfcsYbqxw

Business Models: Online Arbitrage & Wholesale.

Life Success Engineer:
https://www.lifesuccessengineer.com/

Massive Action Academy:
https://www.lifesuccessengineer.com/academy

YouTube Channel: http://lifesuccessengineer.com/youtube

Instagram Page: http://lifesuccessengineer.com/instagram

TRIBE MEMBER 2: DAVID MCGUIGAN

David is a 21-year old online arbitrager that had sold more than £45,000 in 30 Days in Q4 2018. When he was 16 years old, he was a dropout and tried to make money online by buying and selling on eBay and Amazon. He had success with both platforms, but currently focusing on Amazon. He has recently moved into his warehouse and pushing his business to even bigger heights.

How has a failure or apparent failure, set you up for later success? Do you have a "favourite failure" of yours?

I was initially selling on eBay. I was trading there and then last year I was involved in dealing with illegitimate people who were using credit card fraud. The police thought it was me so they came to my house and started an investigation. They took my laptop during the time I was in Thailand when I heard the news from my family. It really struck me.

Luckily, I had been documented on Instagram and had found other people in our community. When I came back from Thailand, I wasn't doing much through my days and was stressed. I found some amazing content on YouTube and from that point, I decided to give Amazon FBA a go. I've learned a lot and went for it.

What is one of the best or most worthwhile investments you've ever made? (Could be time, money, energy etc.)

I think it has to be the London meet up I went to earlier in 2018. I wasn't sure what to expect at the meetup and when I got there I realized that quite a lot of people knew about my story because I was documenting it, which was amazing.

There's such an incredible value in meeting people in real life because you get to connect with them and learn directly from them.

In the last 5 years, what new belief, behaviour, or habit has most improved your life?

I'm trying to stop caring about what anyone or everyone thinks. It's just like a mindset switch. Once I've started to try and remove the thoughts in my head of what might this person think, or what my mom or friends think, it just opened up so many opportunities.

I've still got a little way to go and I get a bit anxious about what people think but I'm trying to remove the judgment of others in my head.

What best advice would you give to someone about to enter the world of arbitrage?

My first experience with arbitrage was when I was younger. My sister and I would set up in the garage and sell food and drinks. When I went to school, I was doing a bit of arbitrage. I was buying chocolates and sweets from the shops and trying to sell them to the pupils. I was sort of doing arbitrage naturally but didn't think about that until maybe the past year or two.

My advice for anyone looking to get into arbitrage would be you have to enjoy it because it will be a lot easier. Even if you're not completely in love with the idea of arbitrage, it's a practical way to make money and opportunities are there.

Yes, there are more sellers, but that also means there are more customers.

What are bad recommendations you hear relating to arbitrage?

The idea that it's easy but it's NOT easy. It's simple and it's just like anything else but it involves a lot of hard work.

When you feel overwhelmed or unfocused, or have lost your focus temporarily what do you do?

Set an alarm. Get up early. Go do some exercise. And then, start completing your tasks.

Interview Link: https://youtu.be/G17iSFuxgio

Business Models: Online Arbitrage & Wholesale.

Instagram: https://www.instagram.com/davidmcguigan/

YouTube: https://www.youtube.com/channel/UCr89DSxkpKYGqrh4qcVtKuQ

TRIBE MEMBER 3: SILVIA VENDRAMINETTO

Silvia is an Italian living in London. She achieved a bachelor's degree in Venice and a masters degree in London. She had worked in the cinema/theatre industry with 20th Century Fox running red carpets for Steven Spielberg and many more. She eventually got burned out and had "enough" of the lobbies of not being able to "grow" and "expand" as much as she wanted due to no-meritocracy. She moved to London and started over as a waitress and eventually became an events manager in the corporate world often being the only woman. She became the only woman foreigner to rise to management levels in the company. She had dreamed about having an online business for years starting eBay while working 70+ hours a week as well as commuting 2.5 hours a day in London. She leaped into fulltime reselling last January 2018. She then started Amazon FBA in mid-July 2018 and building he business to over 6 figures in 6 months.

How has a failure or apparent failure, set you up for later success? Do you have a "favourite failure" of yours?

Oh my God! I have made many choices in my life. I have constantly and consciously got myself out of my comfort zone over and over again. I have learned that what at the beginning seems to be the most unfair situation or a massive failure has always turned out to be the biggest blessing in my life and the universe guiding me to the "right" path.

Yes, I am one of those dream boards/visualisations crazy people. My favourite failure is probably failing the first year of my acting academy at age 19. I wanted it so badly and being kicked out, now looking back, I think saved my future.

What is one of the best or most worthwhile investments you've ever made? (Could be time, money, energy, etc.)

T Harv Eker' s The Millionaire Mind Intensive Workshop in London VIP ticket - where I have also first met Kev three years ago.

UPW London 2018 - Having now a Tony Robbin's Elite Coach in my life.

The first £700 I have invested in my eBay shop.

Writing this down I have realised how all the best money invested has been for my personal growth.

In the last 5 years, what new belief, behaviour, or habit has most improved your life?

1. That Milan, Rome, Venice or London doesn't matter. I will always find beautiful people and awful ones. I will always have new challenges, new homes, new painful experiences, new successes, and that it doesn't mean I will end up losing the other beautiful people that I have already in my life. Now let's work to have the money and the freedom to fly to see them whenever I want to.

2. That this is a REAL business. When you start reselling you can get caught up in the "hobbyist" side income mindset. I have worked hard on this point.

3. That I am a millionaire in the making.

4. That I am great at managing my money and business money.

5. "I don't have money to do it" is bullsh*t. I multiply money is my mantra.

6. It is not perfect because it will never be - and THIS IS OK.

What best advice would you give to someone about to enter the world of arbitrage?

Don't run before you can walk but don't get caught up in the "I need to know it all before I start" or "it needs to be perfect".

Get some experience in complaint management/customer service. This is a business and it is never personal. Deal with it and move on. There are techniques and approaches that you can learn and that will save your time. You will make mistakes. Accept it, forgive yourself as quickly as possible, thank yourself for trying, and move on.

What are bad recommendations you hear relating to arbitrage?

1. You can build an empire working 15 minutes a day.

2. You can build a millionaire business starting with £100 - you can and there are many ways but it is not that straight forward. If I look back I have started with so little and I will get there. The more you invest the quicker you can grow - look up as too fast growth is also one of the main reasons for businesses' failure...

3. Start your journey with private labeling.

4. Invest all your time/money in 1 or 2 products.

In my experience, differentiation is key.

When you feel overwhelmed or unfocused, or have lost your focus temporarily what do you do?

I get up, put some music on, dance, I breathe deeply, drink some water and possibly go for a walk or swim.

GET IT OUT.

Interview Link: https://youtu.be/-yQx8Bxnowl

Business Models: Retail Arbitrage & Online Arbitrage.

Instagram: https://www.instagram.com/silvia_toughhumans/

TRIBE MEMBER 4: ADAM KUPINSKI

Adam had worked as a lorry driver and he went on to running the transport office for a couple of years. He always felt he wanted more for his family. He wanted to have his own business and create some sort of legacy. Three years ago, Adam came across a perfect business model, Online Arbitrage.

Amazingly, Adam built his business to over £47,000 in 30 days in Q4 in 2018 and going on to 7 figures in total revenue throughout his journey.

How has a failure or apparent failure, set you up for later success? Do you have a "favourite failure" of yours?

My favourite one was building this online arbitrage business where I wasn't using a Repricer. This resulted in up to £12,000 in sales. That was just simply down to the fact that I just didn't know that the tool existed.

I've set myself to learn as much as I could about this model and I will never stop. There's always something you can learn and tweak in your procedures to make more profit.

What is one of the best or most worthwhile investments you've ever made? (Could be time, money, energy etc.)

There are two of them that made a massive impact on my life.

First is reading books, not the fiction ones, but those that expand or change your mindset. Rich Dad, Poor Dad by Robert Kiyosaki is one of them. My goal is actually to read as much as I possibly can in my spare time.

Second is actually what happened to me in 2018 when I joined Kev's Success Partnership and you wouldn't believe how much of an impact that had on my business. I think it was in the middle of August when we had our first session, but before that, I was struggling to get to 15 or £16,000 in sales. A week after that coaching call, I went to about £22,000 in sales. That's an almost 50% increase. Then onto nearly £50,000 in 30 days as well.

I strongly suggest investing in a business coach because you don't know what sort of impact it can make for your business.

In the last 5 years, what new belief, behaviour, or habit has most improved your life?

As I've said, I used to work for someone else and even though I was always good at it, I felt like this is not what I want to do. I was always looking for an opportunity and the biggest thing that happened was a shift in my mindset. It was a simple saying to myself, "Oh yes, I can do it."

What best advice would you give to someone about to enter the world of arbitrage?

Don't get subscribed to too many groups. What you'll find quite often is that you'll get conflicting points of view and it will just leave you confused and you will not know what action to do.

So, the best thing I would suggest is to find someone who actually does what you would like to do and you resonate with their message and just stick with them.

What are bad recommendations you hear relating to arbitrage?

I think the worst one I could probably hear is that this business model is way too overcrowded.

There's plenty of space for new sellers. There are projections that Amazon is going to grow about 15 to 20 per cent a year over the next ten years. Don't get put off with what you hear that there are already thousands of sellers.

When you feel overwhelmed or unfocused, or have lost your focus temporarily what do you do?

That happens quite often. So, for me, the best way is to get out and clear your mind. I read a book, go for a walk, and think through the problem and see new ways of dealing with it or think about who I can reach out to for help.

Whatever works for you, it can be going to the gym or having a bit of time to think through it and then take massive action.

Interview Link: https://youtu.be/lvEVjsPV2Ng

Business Models: Online Arbitrage & Wholesale.

Facebook: https://www.facebook.com/adamkupinski

TRIBE MEMBER 5: JAKE DIEGO

Happily married, father of two, and living in the US Midwest all his life. He heard about Amazon during a speech a friend was giving where she shared that every time she buys something on Amazon, she always clicks 'used and new - other offers' and that led Jake down a wild path to where he is now.

Jake has now quit his job, and amazingly in Q4 in 2018, he sold over $63,000 in 30 days while still being full time employed.

How has a failure or apparent failure, set you up for later success? Do you have a "favourite failure" of yours?

I've failed a lot with various multi-level marketing organizations (Nutrilite & Melaleuca), I put becoming a landlord on hold, and trading stocks and options.

My favourite failure is trading stocks and options I learned the most from it although I also lost the most money that was about $5,000. I learned how to read charts, market dynamics, trends, and have a longer-term outlook.

I now only invest for dividends and industries with growth potential.

What is one of the best or most worthwhile investments you've ever made? (Could be time, money, energy etc.)

Learning to let go. It sounds kind of hippy but it's been one of the most valuable things I've ever learned.

It allows me to not make decisions based on my biases, preconceived notions, and opinions. In short, a lot of habits, choices, and everyday things we do are patterns, we've learned from our parents, siblings, and close relatives/friends. That's not an issue in itself but not all of them are serving you towards achieving your goals in life.

By letting go, we can access our intuitive knowingness and clear reason and that's when life gets amazing.

In the last 5 years, what new belief, behaviour, or habit has most improved your life?

Breaking down goals into smaller steps. Don't tackle a goal as a big hairy, scary thing. Break it down and decide which milestones need to be achieved as you move in that direction.

For example, if you have an annual goal - what do you need to do in 6 months, 3 months, 1 month, 2 weeks? Then write it out and revisit it regularly to track your progress or lack of progress and make adjustments.

What best advice would you give to someone about to enter the world of arbitrage?

Be patient. These things will take time and your going to lose money. Your sales will build over time. Keep learning and if you have a question, always ask.

What are bad recommendations you hear relating to arbitrage?

Do not buy a product to sell from eBay. Amazon will suspend you.

Do not place store orders with large quantities of the same item. Make yourself look like a regular customer.

Do not drop ship. It's the fastest way to suspension.

Do not post any customer information publicly. Remember, all Amazon Seller messages are monitored.

When you feel overwhelmed or unfocused, or have lost your focus temporarily what do you do?

Take a break. Depending on the urgency of something, this maybe 5 minutes or the rest of the day.

Interview Link: https://youtu.be/lvEVjsPV2Ng

Business Models: Retail Arbitrage & Online Arbitrage.

Instagram: https://www.instagram.com/jake._diego/

YouTube: https://www.youtube.com/user/ImprovingYourImpact

TRIBE MEMBER 6: DEVAN JORDAN

Dev is 21 years old, he dropped out of university and the normal route of society to chase his dream of being in charge of his future and now a year and a half later, he runs a 6-figure Amazon FBA business with a warehouse and employees in-house and around the world.

How has a failure or apparent failure, set you up for later success? Do you have a "favourite failure" of yours?

The failure of starting the Amazon business and stopping it. We started Amazon FBA 6 months or so before we started this business and it was while I was still at university. I would mainly do Retail Arbitrage and drive home with a full car each weekend to go home, prep items, send them and get back to University on Monday. I then had a choice to make as the workload at university was increasing and I decided to fail the Amazon business, sell everything and move onto university fully.

I was very unhappy at university and was looking for any kind of escape to make myself happy showed me a way that was possible, it had worked before when I put only 2 days of effort into it so why not start it properly and smash it out the park. Something that I never went onto regret and never will.

What is one of the best or most worthwhile investments you've ever made? (Could be time, money, energy etc.)

The best investment I have made without a doubt will be the time and energy I have put and continue to put into making my vision come true.

I spend all day and night either working on or thinking about this business and my next move. Whereas previously, I spent 2 days a week, I now spend 7 days a week which shocks a lot of people when I tell them or they get told but I am so dedicated to making this work not only for me but for the future of my family that I don't want to put my time into anything else.

While some people when they receive this freedom of having no boss or shift time would maybe socialise a lot more and go out more I do less. No shift means I can work whenever I want which means 6 am, 2 pm, 8 pm, 1 am or all of the above. I try to work on this business until my mind is physically drained and then I go home to bed and sit and think about what I'm going to do the next day.

A quote that sticks with me is I believe Elon Musk saying if I work 60-100 hours a week I can get done in 20 years what it would take someone 40 to do.

In the last 5 years, what new belief, behaviour, or habit has most improved your life?

This is the thought process of not giving a second thought to what people think of you in anything you do.

I was never hugely bothered about looking nice clothes-wise and having the biggest brands but I'm even less so now in that I wear joggers, hoody and pink fluffy socks to work every day.

Another huge example of when not caring is starting this job fulltime. If any of you reading this are Amazon sellers, you will understand the stigma around it. We have a joke in our group that people call it 'that Amazon thing' and don't see it as a proper business model when we are out here making more money per year than a lot of shops in our town.

So, I am very much feeling strong in that anything I am doing or going to do as long as it brings me happiness and doesn't bring anyone else's sadness than that is what I will do regardless of what people think of it. I wouldn't be writing this now if I cared.

What best advice would you give to someone about to enter the world of arbitrage?

The advice that I give anyone that asks me on Instagram and also anyone that I mentor is not only the previous statement of not caring what people think but also never give up. As you've read, I gave up on Amazon back when I thought university was the right thing but if I had not given up that who knows what stage I would be at now.

Also, a lot of people start blind and wonder why the hell they can't find these products that make money because it looks so easy on people's Instagram. It's not easy to take your time, ask, learn and keep at it. You will get to the place you want to get to. You may fail a few times. It might be that you buy some products that make you take a loss or your account may get suspended, it doesn't matter. There is a resolution to everything and just remember the reason why you started.

NEVER GIVE UP.

What are bad recommendations you hear relating to arbitrage?

You may see a lot all over your Instagram feed and Facebook feed people posing with Ferrari's and the title being do you want to make 100k in 24 hours. This is the worst recommendation about arbitrage in that you can get rich quick.

There are a lot of courses out there and some of them are like this and it's most likely going to be the ones you see a lot of because they spend a lot on advertisements.

You cannot get rich quick from Online Arbitrage FACT.

These people who tell you that you can have probably either got lucky or put a lot of effort in and are now trying to persuade you to give them more money so they increase their wealth. There are however lots of truthful and genuine change that the life courses you invested in can help you a lot. Just be careful.

When you feel overwhelmed or unfocused, or have lost your focus temporarily what do you do?

I am quite lucky in that I don't usually feel overwhelmed by pressure and I can usually handle any kind of workload as I have learned to micromanage. Something I was very good at university but it just shows the difference when you enjoy something.

Lately, however, since hiring my sister who with the wages we pay her keeps a roof over her's and my nieces head as well as playing with my grandparent's money and if anything goes wrong I'm to blame. I have been feeling quite a bit of pressure and for the first time in years I have felt stressed but the one thing that keeps me focused on what I need to do is the reason I am here and where I have been.

Stacking shelves at Tesco, sat in a lecture theatre falling to sleep, having a job driving around the country and being close to fatally crashing many times. These are the reasons, which help me get focused and do what I need to do because I don't want to go back to those places. This is my time and i will do what I need to do.

Interview Link: https://youtu.be/SQ4dRanbjVs

Business Models: Online Arbitrage & Wholesale.

Instagram: http://instagram.com/DEVANJORDANfba/

YouTube: https://www.youtube.com/channel/UCqiiEMYbbvzLpSm00dlZl2w

TRIBE MEMBER 7: CHRIS ELSEY

A dad of 1 and a budding entrepreneur, Chris had worked in IT for 18 years and had been running his own Amazon FBA business for almost 4 years. He continues to learn every day and follow his dreams.

How has a failure or apparent failure, set you up for later success? Do you have a "favourite failure" of yours?

I took on an affiliate website about 10 years ago. I bought it for £600. It was claimed to be making £900 per month. The guy who sold it to me was using a banner network to advertise and there was no space available. Basically, I'd spend £600 on a website that had no chance. Today, though, I understand more about websites and how to drive free traffic, etc.

I've actually got another website now that's totally unrelated to Amazon and has got lots of articles and useful information. It receives daily targeted traffic from Google, so there's no paid traffic, no banner networks, no PPC, nothing going on other than sort of free traffic.

What is one of the best or most worthwhile investments you've ever made? (Could be time, money, energy etc)

Without any shadow of a doubt, it's investing in the Amazon course that Andy runs in London. I've made my investment back time and time again.

In the last 5 years, what new belief, behaviour, or habit has most improved your life?

The belief that anything is possible and that there are no limits.

I came from a working class background where everybody was quite negative. The belief that my parents taught me and that their parents taught them was that the rich gets richer and the poor gets poorer.

But, I came across personal development coaches like Bob Proctor and Tony Robbins. I started watching a lot of their videos and studying a lot of what they were saying and they just blew my mind.

It's the law of attraction where everything is energy and everything vibrates.

What best advice would you give to someone about to enter the world of arbitrage?

Reinvest ALL profits early on; diversify your stock lines by going shallow and wide. Document everything. It's absolutely critical to make sure that you've accounted for everything. Share the buy box. Spend time understanding Keepa, this will pay off in the future. Be prepared to learn a lot and focus on one thing first then move to something else.

What are bad recommendations you hear relating to arbitrage?

Price wars and general undercutting.

It's terrible advice and should always be avoided. It just depletes profits and no one wins. Something that's not always widely talked about is the expense that comes with the business. Accountant's fees, software fees, prep fees, Amazon fees.

Don't let this put off at all but just be aware of them.

When you feel overwhelmed or unfocused, or have lost your focus temporarily what do you do?

I generally listen to motivational music or play a motivational video on YouTube. Staying positive and watching/following personal development influencers speakers is so important. My personal favourites are Bob Proctor, Tony Robbins, and Jim Rohn.

I actually have a playlist on Spotify and it's called Millionaire. I've got sort of music in there and songs that when I listed to this playlist, I sort of visualise them and imagine myself being this millionaire. Trust me, it gets you in the right frame of mind.

Interview Link: https://youtu.be/LLqM_1XzhcM

Business Models: Online Arbitrage & Wholesale.

Facebook: https://facebook.com/groups/ArbitrageSuperstars/

YouTube: https://youtube.com/arbitragesuperstars

TRIBE MEMBER 8: ELLIOT STOUTT

Elliott is 26 years old and from Leeds. He is a fulltime head of the P.E. department in a secondary school and a part-time bookseller on Amazon FBA, which he has been doing for more than two years already. He spends his weekends going out, scanning books, and shipping them out to Amazon.

He has grown such an amazing following on his Instagram account which is his main social platform. His purpose is to empower and inspire people to start selling on Amazon because it's an incredible way to make a semi-passive income. You can take it easy like you can do it one day or two days and eventually you can do it fulltime.

How has a failure or apparent failure, set you up for later success? Do you have a "favourite failure" of yours?

A lot of people are like "I do not like failure". However, though it sounds very cliché, the pain of failure even pushes me further.

I remember when I first started I was very naive and when people first start, they buy every book going. The lower the sales rank, the better the product sells. So, I was going out there and buying books that were maybe ranked at 5 million, 6 million, 800,000. I bought all these products and eventually got stung with long-term storage fees and the amount was crazy. It kind of set me back a little bit and I had to think in my head if this is really something that I want to do.

So, I adapted this business model and instead of buying in bulk, store on the shelf and hope for the best, I actually went through more like a cherry-picking style because that suited me now.

I really love now going into shops and even if I buy two to three to five books in a shop, they're going to be top-notch. The sales rank is going to be amazing. I'm going to have no competition. Amazon has run out of stock. There's no FBA seller. Merchant sellers might be selling them for £50 and I can sell it for more.

So, that failure from that long-term storage fee really kind of inspired me to think and sit down and go through what I actually wanted from the process of Amazon.

What is one of the best or most worthwhile investments you've ever made? (Could be time, money, energy etc.)

I would say it would be reading books. I started reading graciously about three years ago and the best book I've ever bought was Tim Ferriss' Tools of Titans. It got loads of successful people, whether it be health, mind, spirit, and financial, who answered about eight questions with their secrets. How amazing is it that we can access the minds of a hundred to two hundred successful people and know what they do and what makes them successful now.

Morning rituals, 12-minute HIT training, and listening to podcasts are also among my best investments.

In the last 5 years, what new belief, behaviour, or habit has most improved your life?

Morning rituals are a massive one. I've also got a night routine where literally no phones after 9:30. I have a cold shower, piano music that chills me out, lighted candles, and read to settle me down and reduce cortisol levels.

I've also started meditating. After working out at the gym, I sit in the car and do the meditation. So, literally physical and mental workout.

Vishen Lakhiani's book The Extraordinary Mind is a recommended one where he talks about the six phase meditation: relax time, vision time, time to forgive people, being grateful for the things, and then you go home and feel better.

What best advice would you give to someone about to enter the world of arbitrage?

The hardest thing to do in anything is starting because the brain wants to protect you. It doesn't want you to step out of comfort zones.

And, you've got to fight against your brain in this one. There are a number of outlets that you can use now to start and help you to start.

So, ask questions to people. Download the seller app and just start scanning books and get used to the process of Amazon. Look at YouTube videos to help you with online arbitrage.

What are bad recommendations you hear relating to arbitrage?

When people follow and look at other people's accomplishments, this really frustrates me. As a beginner, some are looking at the 6-figure earners and are like "how come I'm not like that and I'm not hitting my targets".

Be realistic. Take it day-by-day, step-by-step. Ask questions. Stay humble and just kind of enjoy the process. Stop comparing yourself to the Joneses of Amazon.

When you feel overwhelmed or unfocused, or have lost your focus temporarily what do you do?

This week has been quite difficult. It's exam season at the moment in school. There's a lot of pressure and a lot of hoops to jump through. And, I have become very not unfocused, in fact, I've become so focused that I've nearly burnt out. And, I think what most people do is pretend that everything's okay.

But you know what, sometimes it's okay not to be okay.

It's just about adjusting your mental well-being. And, first things first, above everything, above making money on Amazon, health is the number one priority.

So, I take a couple of days off, breathe a little bit, spend some time with the people that matter to me, and write down affirmations.

Interview Link: https://youtu.be/-G2C5jpqtuE

Business Models: Books.

Instagram: https://www.instagram.com/fbajourney/

TRIBE MEMBER 9: JON CASE

Jon started his Amazon selling business in 2016. He sells used books and does it all with a suitcase.

How has a failure or apparent failure, set you up for later success? Do you have a "favourite failure" of yours?

Before Amazon, I had side hustles, had a job and internet marketing. I tried all that stuff like selling affiliate products like how to quit smoking and I've never smoked in my whole life, and how to fix a relationship even though being single for two years. They didn't quite work out and I had no passion for them. From those mistakes I learned how to do Facebook pages linked to blogs, Twitter, and all this stuff.

I was thinking I'm just going to focus on what I enjoy and I enjoy reading personal development books.

Another thing is that before doing the FBA, I was doing property with the no to little money and stuff but later down the line you'd still need money. I was trying to do everything.

I realised I needed to focus on my strengths and stop trying to fix my weaknesses.

What is one of the best or most worthwhile investments you've ever made? (Could be time, money, energy etc.)

I would say when I started reading the book Rich Dad, Poor Dad. I've read it three times while I was travelling. On the third time, I was like oh my gosh right, and it also taught me that I don't know anything yet.

In the last 5 years, what new belief, behaviour, or habit has most improved your life?

For the first time in my life, I joined a gym. I usually do workouts at home. I realised I have myself to tell myself to go. It's just been getting up and being more driven in the day.

The second thing would be a mind shift. Before, I was just chasing money but I asked myself what is it that I really want. I just want to laugh as much as I can and that's it. I just felt like a weight was lifted.

What best advice would you give to someone about to enter the world of arbitrage?

Just start. A lot of people overthink and see arbitrage as if they were in a cliff and thus stop themselves. So, it's kind of like just take that leap.

The second thing is to always review your business and don't be afraid to test new things. It's also like testing yourself on what works for you. Review all the pricing, the ranks, and really study the ins and outs.

What are bad recommendations you hear relating to arbitrage?

People buy new stuff on eBay and sell on Amazon and people complain about all these and ask for receipts. EBay is like the wild wild west and does not have valid invoice.

Also, don't sell a book new if you bought it in charity even if it's sealed and looks new. Amazon will chase you up.

When you feel overwhelmed or unfocused, or have lost your focus temporarily what do you do?

Two things: either sleep or dance.

I recently posted on Instagram and it was like when all else fails, I just like to take a nap. I like sleeping. It's just like you're tired sometimes and overworked. When I first fulltime, I was like hustle, hustle, hustle. I was passing out. When I got a night of sleep, I'm more focused on my work.

I also dance and just chill like everyone's rolling on the floor and be weird.

Interview Link: https://youtu.be/yBh0q1cDgJQ

Business Models: Books.

Instagram: https://www.instagram.com/thejcfiles/

TRIBE MEMBER 10: ANDY LAWRENCE

Andy has been an Amazon & eBay Wholesale Reseller for over 10 Years, Owner of the Wholesale Help community and Travel addict. He builds his online businesses to fuel his passion for world travel and personal connection.

How has a failure or apparent failure, set you up for later success? Do you have a "favourite failure" of yours?

There is always a positive outcome for me after each failure because I will try to learn how to do it better next time. I could not have made half the wholesale deals I have over the years if I hadn't been told no a hundred times. The crucial thing is to try and find the reason for each no and then you will never lose because you can improve each time.

Each no is another piece of the puzzle, a little more insight, a little closer to a yes. If the end goal is worth it then a hundred no's is a small price to pay. Embrace failure as part of the journey and you will achieve so much more.

What is one of the best or most worthwhile investments you've ever made? (Could be time, money, energy etc.)

The best investment has to be the warehouse. As you scale your business, space is usually the biggest bottleneck and to be able to grow, you need the right resources to make it happen. It also gives you the credibility with the Wholesale suppliers that you are serious and will help get the deals done.

In the last 5 years, what new belief, behaviour, or habit has most improved your life?

Self-awareness and self-improvement have made a big difference in my life and continues to do so, being able to understand your strengths and weaknesses will help you become far more productive and generally be more present as you go through life. I take time out to work on my own personal skills and learn new ways to be a better human. It is probably the most important work you can do.

What best advice would you give to someone about to enter the world of arbitrage?

Become a scholar of the data, learn to read it like Neo in The Matrix! When you really understand the way stock sells and how the Keepa data looks and flows, you will always have an edge over your competition and can work around the penny undercutters. Take the time to watch how the best seller rank changes over time and how much it moves in particular categories when you really understand it's like buying profit!

What are bad recommendations you hear relating to arbitrage?

You have to be the cheapest to make sales. WRONG! If you use Repricer software, you can set it to MATCH the competition not undercut by a penny. You can do the whole reseller community and yourself a great favour if you match your competition. You will still sell your stock but you will also keep the profits up without initiating a pointless downward spiral. Don't give in to fear a stupidity.

When you feel overwhelmed or unfocused, or have lost your focus temporarily what do you do?

First off, exercise is key. If you're in a rut, distracted or overwhelmed, change the environment straight away. Take a walk in the fresh air, go for a swim, a run, whatever is your exercise of choice just get the blood moving. It will re-oxygenate your brain. Take your mind away from what is causing the issue and when you get back to it, you will have a fresh approach and more energy to tackle it.

If you are dealing with a large task, you need to break it right down into it's smallest components and just do the first part of it, making progress is key however small. Once you complete a part of it you will build momentum and get that feeling of accomplishment back and you're off and running again.

Interview Link: https://youtu.be/8dxOMxsobDQ

Business Models: Wholesale.

YouTube: https://www.youtube.com/andy0lawrence

Instagram: https://www.instagram.com/wholesale_help/

TRIBE MEMBER 11: LUKE FILER

At age 10 I did 3 figure sales running a second hand shop. At the age of 21 I've hit 6 figure sales on Amazon.

On the 20th February 1998 I was born in South Africa as the only child in our Family. 2 years later my younger brother joined us. At age 5, we moved to the United Kingdom, where I still live today.

After finishing school with some excellent A-Levels, I fulfilled a long-term goal and spent 6 months living, and playing cricket, in Australia.

Back in the UK, I began studying Accounting and Finance at the University of Leeds.

Throughout my life I have had various entrepreneurial adventures. However, my first "proper" business venture began in the summer of 2018 when I made my first sale on Amazon.

Help from others has been a huge part in my success. I am extremely grateful of this and therefore I have setup the iGen Entrepreneur brand to allow me to help others starting their journey.

University lasted until April 2019, when I dropped out to pursue my Amazon business full time.

Going forward I will continue to scale the Amazon business. My passion for travel means I will be visiting South Africa, Botswana, SE Asia, Australia and the USA over the next 9 months.

How has a failure or apparent failure, set you up for later success? Do you have a "favourite failure" of yours?

I think most people would consider dropping out of University a failure. In fact, when I tell people who ask how Uni is going, 90% of them say sorry and seem to feel bad for asking.

I think this "failure" has already allowed me to develop my business massively.

Without dropping out I wouldn't have been able to hire and train the 6 VAs currently working for me. Or at least, I wouldn't be at the stage I'm currently at. As well as this, I wouldn't have been able to attend the Amafest event where I met some awesome people.

I strongly believe I've learned far more running a business than I have from University.

What is one of the best or most worthwhile investments you've ever made? (Could be time, money, energy etc.)

Any Amazon related event I've been to purely for the networking. I believe strongly that relationships are the key to everything.

In the last 5 years, what new belief, behaviour, or habit has most improved your life?

Going to the gym. It's something I've wanted to do but never got started. Now I have a routine that I keep up.

Also on routines, I've started waking up earlier. Last summer I was often waking up midday/early afternoon. Now I am waking up earlier and feeling better. It's also important to be awake when the rest of the world is working at times!

What best advice would you give to someone about to enter the world of arbitrage?

Document your journey. Not just to see your progress etc, but also to document processes you use. Hopefully you get to the stage where you want to outsource your business and if you have these processes documented, it will be a lot easier.

Selling in UK marketplace: Be aware of European Fulfilment Network fees!

What are bad recommendations you hear relating to arbitrage?

The 3x rule... source based on finding items that sell for 3 times the cost.

When you feel overwhelmed or unfocused, or have lost your focus temporarily what do you do?

Have a shower. It's refreshing and a great place to take a step back and put things into perspective. Whether this be realising how lucky I am in terms of my overall life position, or even just putting small "problems" into perspective in terms of thinking: "How will this effect me over the next 5 years".

Interview Link: https://youtu.be/fdymSZ1zNvo

Business Models: Online Arbitrage.

Facebook Group: https://www.facebook.com/groups/iGenEntrepreneur/

YouTube: https://www.youtube.com/channel/UCtaJGE3Kuk4QaWXei9ujbDQ

TRIBE MEMBER 12: REEZY RESELLS

Michael Rezendes II better known as Reezy Resells having been a high school drop out and government assistance recipient to now selling over $5 million in lifetime sales on Amazon. He began documenting and sharing his journey with the public in order to inspire thousands of people world wide to "follow the hustle" and escaping the rat race.

How has a failure or apparent failure, set you up for later success? Do you have a "favourite failure" of yours?

I never thought I could automate the sourcing aspect of my business. I was forced to re evaluate that when I broke my foot. I decided to train and hire someone. Because of the adversity of facing that challenge it provided the same type of pressure that failure does to me. Failure or adversity can force you to operate in a different mindset or perspective. Sometimes a setback or failure can set you up for a future success.

What is one of the best or most worthwhile investments you've ever made? (Could be time, money, energy etc.)

Hiring employees to scale my business. You can build an empire out of the investment out of a good employees.

In the last 5 years, what new belief, behaviour, or habit has most improved your life?

As resellers we often think about how much we are going to make, but what are we will to lose. Always have a exit loss strategy.

What best advice would you give to someone about to enter the world of arbitrage?

You need to learn how to do completed searches on eBay. Learn how to use the amazon seller app. Learn how to use the platforms and process. Don't focus on the profits at first. You have to have a hunger to learn. Minimize your risk by selling used first.

What are bad recommendations you hear relating to arbitrage?

Getting ungated vs proving authenticity of items

You CAN use retail receipts to prove authenticity if you get a claim against you.

You cannot use retail receipts to get ungated.

When you feel overwhelmed or unfocused, or have lost your focus temporarily what do you do?

- Writing gratitude

- Exercise

- Listening to motivation

- Seeing the success of others

Interview Link: https://youtu.be/VtxN_g8nCgQ

Business Models: Books & Retail Arbitrage.

YouTube: https://www.youtube.com/channel/UCeq8GxD-kFVV5S1i0MCmzTg

Instagram: https://www.instagram.com/reezyresells/

TRIBE MEMBER 13: GARETH THOMAS

My name is Gareth Thomas I have been selling on Amazon since 2015.

I started by using the Retail Arbitrage Model to begin my journey and still love this model, with £800 on my Credit card. I came from a retail background working in a very well known electrical store progressing into the management team in England and used my knowledge of retail to assist the way I sourced. Then moving into Online Arbitrage, wholesale and Private Label to build my business to where we are today, although Retail Arbitrage still plays a very propionate part of my Amazon Business model. We now operate from a 3000sqft Warehouse I'm also very proud to call Kev Blackburn my Brother after he met my sister Kylie. You can find me on Instagram   @amazonfuelledbysuccess.

How has a failure or apparent failure, set you up for later success? Do you have a "favourite failure" of yours?

So this is a difficult Question I'm taking a different angle of this question but TIME is my favourite failure. What I mean by this is time invested in me or in my business and how I managed it. The way in which it may be classed as a failure is maybe not executing the time available to the best of my ability at the beginning of my business. So I'm quite a social person and when I was trying to balance my friends, full time job and start a new business with family time etc i think the Time split initially maybe was not quite correct ha-ha. I was still enjoying my nights out etc which I still think is a good thing to do every now and then but its finding the right balance from those experiences which has helped me to learn to become the more productive person and business I run today. It's managing those experiences of trying to have family time versus being productive and getting a business up and running that have helped me to find the right family / friends / and business split from those early mistakes. It can be difficult when starting a business while still working a full time job with a young family and friends to add in the mix but this helped me to become the productive person I am today. So the tip to takeaway that I learnt from all this is planning instead of working off the cuff, planning your days/weeks out means you can be much more productive and Time is no longer my Failure but my strength instead.

What is one of the best or most worthwhile investments you've ever made? (Could be time, money, energy etc.)

For me the answer is Self Development investing in myself with time and energy its reading books and going to events like (Tony Robbins unleash the power) which I recommend.

By investing in my self through self-development that's how I overcame question one ha-ha. Self-development is a MASSIVE part of why I'm where I am now things like planning my time better and consuming more knowledge both in business and from a personal point of view has really helped me. I strongly recommend taking time out to invest in yourself as by doing so you are increasing your chances of success. The age we now live in with access to things like Audio books, YouTube, the internet and events accessible to nearly everyone if you want to learn a new skill like being more productive etc its at your fingertips now which is great.

In the last 5 years, what new belief, behaviour, or habit has most improved your life?

For me the belief was set in place when I was lucky enough to be on my uncle and aunties Yacht in Majorca bobbing up and down on the waves as the sun set and listening to my uncle telling both myself and Kev how they had got to where they are now in there business and personal lives, by working hard and making your own luck and riding any that also comes your way seeing what they have achieved set the belief that if I work hard I can make it and this was a significant day with it being so real and in front of me that this got us looking into entrepreneurship. Also not to sound like a broken record but Planning has been the thing that has most improved my life. I say this because it does not come naturally to me I used to be a more of the cuff type of person which is my natural state but through as mentioned in question 2 self development I have changed my habits by using planning to be more productive both in business and my personal life. Also brining in systems and procedures which when you have Kev as a brother in law is fantastic as his systematic mind has rubbed off on me ha-ha. These are the things that have got me to now where I am today.

What best advice would you give to someone about to enter the world of arbitrage?

There is so many things to say but lets keep this simple I would recommend to look after REPLENISHMENT if you do this correct then your business should do well these items are Winners you don't need to keep finding them, look after them keep them stocked so you don't run out. Check how many you are selling could you sell more if you had more stock? Obviously you keep finding new winners but anyone just starting out or even established look after the replen and it will look after you ha-ha The last thing you want to see is that 0 in stock on a great winner that means your loosing money!! Also use the reports available to you Amazon give you all the Data needed so USE IT! There are more and more reports being added use these to supplement your business and help it grow. Last thing really check the selling listing vs. the purchase item things like weight or bundles can catch out sellers and cause Bad feedback so take that extra time to put procedures in so that even after purchase and it turns up someone else if possible checks this before its sent to Amazon or create your own checklist is another great idea. Iv had listings where the title just says the product so it looks like it's a single but in the bullet points or the description it states pack of 2. Request updates to listings if it's still the same item using seller central.

What are bad recommendations you hear relating to arbitrage?

Ok so again I'm going to flip this a little and talk loans or Amazon Lending this is not financial advice just to be clear but there is so much hype about being offered Amazon Lending or taking any loans to help your business. Just to explain in case your not aware Amazon Lending is by invite only and appears as an offer or if you will a (recommendation) see what id there ha-ha offering you additional capital to use in your business now please do not get me wrong lending can be a fantastic opportunity to grow your business and this is not a don't do it. What I'm saying is do you need it? Used correctly they can be great used unwisely they can ruin your business if not planned and calculated it can lead to a false sense of security and may allow you to spend on things that maybe should not be looked at yet iv heard of a lot of sellers that have fallen fowl of this investing in warehouses extra staff etc too soon. So please make sure you look after any capital invested as its the tail end of paying back to watch out for.

When you feel overwhelmed or unfocused, or have lost your focus temporarily what do you do?

I think initially I tend to NOW take a step back from the situation!! as my natural impulse used to be to attack the situation straight away fire fight if you like just get the situation gone but by rushing in at what cost?, but from experience and learning a lot more with the self development side of things, I think its always good to take a little step back and look at the whole picture. That way you can assess it I love going to the gym or going for a run so that little time away to clear your head rather than rushing in can really help you, so when you come back to look at that challenge you can reassess it and look into how do I get to that end goal? What do i need to do? What sort of resources can I pull in? Can I use the Internet, is there anyone in the community Facebook group/YouTube etc that's gone through this experience that could help? From self-development one of my favourite quotes is we never fail we only learn!! You adapt and that's where you can pull strength from in a different situation.

Interview Link: https://youtu.be/0rGj3oaRp9A

YouTube: https://www.youtube.com/channel/UCpDjGCNeNhDcFyMb01uacXA

Instagram: https://www.instagram.com/amazonfuelledbysuccess/

Website: www.fbaprepfacilityuk.com

TRIBE MEMBER 14: GARETH VASSAY JONES

31, from South Wales. Married with a 4-year-old daughter. Started FBA about 12 months ago. Been reselling for a few years on various platforms. Have gone full time on amazon FBA since May.

How has a failure or apparent failure, set you up for later success? Do you have a "favourite failure" of yours?

Being too comfortable in my comfort zone. Taught me to live life more after taking the leap of faith with FBA. Now I try my best to live outside of my comfort zone where possible.

What is one of the best or most worthwhile investments you've ever made? (Could be time, money, energy etc.)

Myself. The best investment I have made is in property education, particularly a very large investment in an advanced property course, which I started at the start of 2019.

In the last 5 years, what new belief, behaviour, or habit has most improved your life?

Running. Simple. Any mindfulness activity helps me mentally, which in turn helps me in my business. I put running and meditating in the same bracket, as both help me significantly with my mentality and positive mental attitude.

What best advice would you give to someone about to enter the world of arbitrage?

Get all of your accounts in one place or under one name from day one e.g. email address, bank account, credit cards, Google doc account.

What are bad recommendations you hear relating to arbitrage?

90% of FBA stuff you see on Instagram is toxic. A lot of people on IG are just flexing with no context behind numbers they post. Follow people who share numbers, specifically profit figures but at the same time people can be who they want on social media, good and bad. More importantly, follow people who just offer advice for the sake of being nice, with no motif involved.

When you feel overwhelmed or unfocused, or have lost your focus temporarily what do you do?

Take a break. I try to think if somebody wasn't aware of any of my insecurities, problems, pre conceived notions or anything I consider to be stresses etc, and was put into my situation and my body, would they think I had a good or a bad life? That's a good mind-set and a good way to think when you're overwhelmed or struggling. I like it anyway.

Interview Link: https://youtu.be/-Tr6PYSnctw

Business Models: Online Arbitrage.

Instagram: https://www.instagram.com/fbauk_

TRIBE MEMBER 15: MATTHEW ADAMS

Matthew Adams is a fulltime entrepreneur. His hustle began at the age of 8 years old, when his Father purchased x100 clearance teapots. He then came up with a bright idea, loaded up his scooter and sold them door-to-door. Within 5 days he had sold out! He then went onto selling a further x800! He was then featured in their local newspaper as all of the proceeds raised went to the Wigan And Leigh Hospice.

This feeling of empathy for helping others and money passing through his hands has driven him to many business money making ideas! Age 12, while his friends were out playing, he set up a car wash business through their summer holidays. Age 16, he left high school with no qualifications but hunger and drive for making money! He set up his own private label supplement business "RockHard Sports" with a £10,000 turnover in its first 3 months!

Age 20, he formed "2-StrokeMad" buying accident damaged vehicles, repairing them and selling them on eBay. Using his eBay listing knowledge to his advantage, he then went onto becoming a sales manager for x3 of the North West Leading Vehicle Breakers. Some of his biggest achievements have been getting engaged and moving into their new home.

But, his most important has got to be his daughter Robyn born May 2018. There is no greater feeling than hearing your baby's cry for the first time. He is incredibly blessed to have created such a loving family! His future goal(s) is to become financially free. He will create a life that will pay him multiple income streams. This will free up his time to lead him onto his other mission. He wants to help and impact as many people as possible. He gains a deep fulfilment in helping others. He firmly believes the secret to living, is giving.

How has a failure or apparent failure, set you up for later success? Do you have a "favourite failure" of yours?

For me, my life has always been some sort of consistent trial and error. It is how you go about dealing with the stress of failure and turning it into an advantage. I perform at my optimum whenever I am in a high-pressure situation, so giving up and taking the easy route is not an option for me.

You are better to try and fail, than to never try it at all.. "Don't live with any regrets."

I do have a funny story for my most epic failure! I was working for a company called Kirby (really big company in the USA). They sell Hoovers. It was my job to be a call out engineer testing and repairing their faulty Hoovers, selling them the latest model. It was my first week on the job when I was halfway through a service. It was time to bring out the new machine from my van. Now after a while, customers become wise to these tactics and she just would not come out of the kitchen! I had to think of a way that would make it in her best interest to come speak with me, I seen a "save the refugees" (Christian book). So, I began to relate to her speaking about Christianity, when she offered me cup of tea..

I got her up testing the machine showing her how clean her carpets were after trying this new Hoover! So I am choking down my long life milky cup of tea, getting to the point where I am showing her the compressor function. I put the balloon adaptor on the end of the pipe and it literally flied past her head just missing her, all of the dirt that she hovered up was spraying all over her living room. I still had to put her machine back together, discard of this tea and to make sure I didn't forget my new found faith leaflets! HAHAHA!!!

What is one of the best or most worthwhile investments you've ever made? (Could be time, money, energy etc.)

To date, the best financial decision I have ever made is purchasing my home. In April of this year, all my hard work, late nights, working weekends finally paid off! I saved up enough to provide a stable secure home for my family and me.

In the last 5 years, what new belief, behaviour, or habit has most improved your life?

In the last 5-6 years I have discovered the law of attraction; it has completely changed my belief and outlook on life.

Realising that life is happening for you and not against you is a blessing! My daily routine has also played a major role in my success. Priming yourself in a morning is vitally important to accomplishing your tasks and what life throws at you during that day.

What best advice would you give to someone about to enter the world of arbitrage?

The best advice I could give to someone starting online arbitrage is, don't overthink all of the strategies. It can be very daunting and overwhelming when you are first starting out. Focus and take it one step at a time. Finesse and move onto the next step, don't run before you can walk and remember Rome was not built in a day!

What are bad recommendations you hear relating to arbitrage?

The only bad recommendation I hear when it comes to arbitrage is that the back end of a customer who is having to for an item that has limited stock (supply and demand).

The only other issue is I know Amazon has spoken out about sellers doing online arbitrage with them not liking it. It will be interesting to see how they will try to monitor this behaviour.

When you feel overwhelmed or unfocused, or have lost your focus temporarily what do you do?

Whenever I feel overwhelmed, stressed out or unfocused, I split my tasks down to 4 simple steps.

1# I write down my goals that I want to achieve for the day.
2# I think about the reason / purpose of why I want to achieve this.
3# I then write down my outcome.
4# I will come up with a strategy / method of how I am going to get there.

YouTube: https://www.youtube.com/channel/UC_cCB2pXznzgM77h6qRJ2vw

Business Models: Used Games/DVD's & Online Arbitrage.

TRIBE MEMBER 16: RAY NATION

Ray grew up in the suburbs of London and was happy plodding along for many years as a London Taxi driver, trading his time for money. Then, Uber came along and immediately affected the amount of money that he was earning, for the worse. He had to think of what he would do to earn more money, as he had bills to pay. Since getting finding Kev online, I have began building my business and making it happen.

How has a failure or apparent failure, set you up for later success? Do you have a "favourite failure" of yours?

When I was a teenager, I was asked by a family friend to work on their fruit and veg stall on Saturdays dealing with the public. I refused because the thought of dealing with money and the public terrified me. I had the "I can't do it" mindset back then, now I've turned it into the "How can I do it?" mindset and I've overcome many obstacles by thinking this way. Many times, the answer is to find people that have done the thing that you want to do, and then model them to learn how.

What is one of the best or most worthwhile investments you've ever made? (Could be time, money, energy etc)

The best investment that I've made has been in myself, changing my mindset by mixing with winners and reading about how winners became winners.

In the last 5 years, what new belief, behaviour, or habit has most improved your life?

I am still working on it, but becoming organised, working on the most important thing and not getting distracted.

What best advice would you give to someone about to enter the world of arbitrage?

Don't spend too long learning all the info before you take massive action. Join the community via the Facebook group and learn from others mistakes. Get Ungated in some categories, so you can sell a more varied amount.

What are bad recommendations you hear relating to arbitrage?

You can make 7 figures within 6 months, with minimum effort...if you buy my course!

When you feel overwhelmed or unfocused, or have lost your focus temporarily what do you do?

I have my list of "Whys" that I read to myself, this really motivates me.

Business Models: Online Arbitrage.

TRIBE MEMBER 17: LARRY LUBARSKY

Larry Lubarsky is an eCommerce entrepreneur and 8-figure Amazon seller. From Brooklyn NY, Larry started an Amazon business through a small loan from a friend and with hard work and talent turned that into a multi-million dollar Amazon wholesale business.

A child of immigrants, Larry was born and raised in Brooklyn, NY. At 16, Larry dropped out of high school and spent the next 15 years "working for the man" in the financial services industry. After hitting rock bottom in 2012 and accumulating over 6 figures in debt, he had finally had enough and decided it was time for a change. Taking on a small business loan from a friend, Larry started an e-commerce business on Amazon.

Finally, finding his true passion after all these years, he worked day & night and turned that small loan into a massive business doing over 8 figures in annual revenue. In 2017, Larry started documenting his day-to-day business on social media @WatchMeAmazon where he gives followers a behind-the-scenes look at an Amazon business, and helps others get started down the e-commerce path.

How has a failure or apparent failure, set you up for later success? Do you have a "favourite failure" of yours?

Failure and rebuilding are part of life. Every time I've had a set back and would have to rebuild, I always came back stronger. This is especially true in the Amazon business where we constantly have to deal with issues and problems. While many sellers may not have the fortitude to survive and are weeded out, the ones that do most often reap the rewards of a long term flourishing Amazon business.

My favourite failure is when I first started selling on Amazon, I was working for someone on a commission basis. They tried to take advantage of that and screw me over. At the time I was pissed, but had they not done that I would have never branched out on my own and open my own eCommerce business.

What is one of the best or most worthwhile investments you've ever made? (Could be time, money, energy etc.)

Working day and night around the clock when I first got into the business. The business is always getting harder to a certain extent and you want to get it while the getting is good.

Next year you will always say "I wish I worked harder last year". Don't!

In the last 5 years, what new belief, behaviour, or habit has most improved your life?

Implementing the RPM goal/life/time management system from Tony Robbins.

What best advice would you give to someone about to enter the world of arbitrage?

I am a big Floyd Mayweather fan for a reason. His motto of "HARDWORK / DEDICATION" rings especially true to those looking to build a business on Amazon.

What are bad recommendations you hear relating to arbitrage?

Too many to list honestly, but never take advice from someone who isn't where you want to be.

When you feel overwhelmed or unfocused, or have lost your focus temporarily what do you do?

Review my goals.

Instagram: https://www.instagram.com/watchmeamazon

Website: www.wholesaleacademy.com

Business Models: Wholesale

TRIBE MEMBER 18: PAUL HAMPTON

Paul is married to Debbie who is also on the arbitrage journey with him and they have a little dog-called Jillie. They both have fulltime jobs but are fed up of the grind and being told what to do, where to do it, when to do it so they want to get out of the rat race and build a successful business that can allow them to get out of being employed and take back control of their lives and live on their terms.

How has a failure or apparent failure, set you up for later success? Do you have a "favourite failure" of yours?

I had little focus on my career when I was younger as I wanted the "easy life" and was too distracted by other things - I used to play semi-professional football and my career came second to that so I could still go training and play the games.

Also, my personal insecurities (see question 3) contributed to me holding myself back and not being as successful as I feel I could (and should) have been. Now, that is all behind me. I have the drive and focus to be successful and build our life on our terms.

What is one of the best or most worthwhile investments you've ever made? (Could be time, money, energy etc)

Buying our current house - we call it our "forever home" and we absolutely love the house and where we live. We carried out some work last year to build an extension and how it turned out is exactly how we pictured it and more. We come home, get into out little bubble and plan the next move on the empire so we can leave our jobs and take our lives back!

In the last 5 years, what new belief, behaviour, or habit has most improved your life?

I struggle with confidence and assertiveness. Doing my "normal" day job has helped to a point as I need to improve in these areas in order to do my job properly but from when I started doing arbitrage, it has helped with this immeasurably as I am running my own business and I have to get things done in order for it to work and success so I cannot afford to hold back.

It has given me the belief and energy to push on and put the effort in to achieve the results. I used to come in from work and sit in front of the TV but for months now pretty much all my spare time is spent doing arbitrage because I want it to succeed and I also enjoy doing it.

What best advice would you give to someone about to enter the world of arbitrage?

Just go for it!! I spent around 18 months reading and researching it which ultimately resulted in me getting the same information from but from different people - I was looking for that little golden nugget from somebody that was the secret to it all that nobody else has figured out but there isn't such a thing. In the end, I just told myself I either had to do it or forget about it so I just did it! It is a straightforward business model - the quicker you get started, the quicker you learn and develop and become better and more successful.

What are bad recommendations you hear relating to arbitrage?

That it is easy - the more you do it and the more you learn the easier it gets but you have to put the work in to get the results out and get to a point where you can look to automate which is the next goal we are working towards. To penny under reprice - there is no need for it as it totally drives profit down for no reason other than to make a quick buck.

When you feel overwhelmed or unfocused, or have lost your focus temporarily what do you do?

I try and push through - I have a vision board which I put in one of the folders I use daily which reminds me of what I want to achieve and I think about how I want my life to be and getting out of the grind of going to work and living my life on my terms and having my destiny in my own hands. I also look at Kev and other people in a similar position who have succeeded in doing this and aspire to be like them, which also drives me on.

Business Models: Online Arbitrage.

TRIBE MEMBER 19: KRIS McCAULEY

Kris has been selling fulltime since early 2017 and selling online since 2010. He started going to garage sales right out of high school to buy things to sell and now run an online retail business focused on health and beauty!

How has a failure or apparent failure, set you up for later success? Do you have a "favourite failure" of yours?

I have had so many failures and I try to learn as much as I can from them. Recently, a failure that comes to mind that was extremely beneficial and worked out great in the long-term run of things.

One of my main suppliers said that they were going to close down and my business partner, and I realized that we had gotten comfortable and complacent. We then started contacting suppliers and locked down two more suppliers that had better margins for our product lines and they even had more products available.

It was about 48 hours later, we were contacted by our main supplier and they told us they were not closing down and everything was good to go.

What is one of the best or most worthwhile investments you've ever made? (Could be time, money, energy etc.)

I think the best investment I ever made was creating a YouTube channel. In the short time I have been on the platform, I have met so many amazing and motivating individuals.

I often say that I have learned more from my small audience than I have teaching them. Learning to get comfortable behind a camera and build an audience is something that I plan on using in whatever business path I pursue in the future.

In the last 5 years, what new belief, behaviour, or habit has most improved your life?

I think one behaviour and belief that has completely changed my income is how I view my time and prioritizing tasks. Before truly analysing this, I found myself going throughout the day not accomplishing what I would like to get done and not making progress as quickly as I would have liked to.

Now, I structure my days based on weekly goals and I prioritize my tasks based on what will bring back the highest ROI and work my way down.

What best advice would you give to someone about to enter the world of arbitrage?

My best advice for someone doing arbitrage is to go into it with the mindset that you are going to get out of it as soon as possible and move to something that is easier to scale and grow. Arbitrage is hands down one of the best places to find wholesale leads and it is how I found my biggest lead that I have built the majority of my business around. However, I was doing arbitrage for 6 to 7 years before transitioning to the wholesale business model. Had I gone into arbitrage with the mindset of pursuing companies to buy hot selling items in bulk, it would have expedited this entire process.

What are bad recommendations you hear relating to arbitrage?

One bad recommendation I hear about arbitrage is to always be sourcing. I think this is true to some extent but the number one priority should be getting out the inventory that has already been sourced.

Time is money and every day, the inventory is sitting and not available for sale is money being lost. A good example of someone putting this into practice video by the bearded picker where he went around to 17 Walmarts in 24 hours buying one particular item and what stood out was that he was actually listing the items as merchant fulfilled on the way back to his car. By the end of the drive, he had already sold 130 items before sending them into Amazon.

When you feel overwhelmed or unfocused, or have lost your focus temporarily what do you do?

This was something that I had trouble with in my first year of entrepreneurship but now I have systems in place to help me get back on track that I like to think of as fail-safes.

My first fail-safe is to take the day off and to not think about work. Sometimes, when I start asking myself questions like "What is the point of what I am doing?" or "What am I even doing with my life?" I know I need to take a step back. The next day I work, I gather all of the tasks that I can do just via laptop and work from my favourite coffee shop to just get the dopamine flowing again! When I have a really bad day though and things seem like events cannot get any worse, I listen to David Goggins nonstop until I realize that my problems could always get worse and that I can conquer anything. There were only 2 times in 2018 I had to do this.

Interview Link: https://youtu.be/EadZsAFarf4

YouTube: https://www.youtube.com/krismccauley

Facebook: https://www.facebook.com/groups/KrisAmazonCommunity/

Business Models: Wholesale & Online Arbitrage.

TRIBE MEMBER 20: ANDY RADE

Andy has been reselling on eBay since 2011. He started Reselling on Amazon in 2018. His goal is to become a full-time Reseller from January 2019. He also teaches Salsa classes in his hometown of Hull.

How has a failure or apparent failure, set you up for later success? Do you have a "favourite failure" of yours?

A few. There has been a time when I had so little money from trying to keep my business afloat that I was living on plain bread and ketchup.

What is one of the best or most worthwhile investments you've ever made? (Could be time, money, energy etc.)

In 2018 I've made an increasing effort to meet other resellers, attend conferences. Money and Time very well spent. It has shown me how to scale my business and to be more open-minded.

In the last 5 years, what new belief, behaviour, or habit has most improved your life?

Hard work is a must. Constant work and learning need to be consistent to get me going to where I want to go in my business life. I know from personal experience. Around 5 years ago, I believed 4 hours a day was enough to keep my business flowing. That kind of thinking put me in a lot of trouble at the time. I simply wasn't investing enough time and energy.

What best advice would you give to someone about to enter the world of arbitrage?

Take your time. Do all the steps required. Don't look for shortcuts. You'll have a much deeper understanding of how it all works as you keep progressing.

What are bad recommendations you hear relating to arbitrage?

That it's easy and can be done easily using 3rd party software.

When you feel overwhelmed or unfocused, or have lost your focus temporarily what do you do?

Get up early in the morning. Meditate for at least 10 minutes. Write do a to-do list of important tasks. Once out of my head and on a piece of paper. I can start to work through them.

Business Models: Books & Online Arbitrage.

TRIBE MEMBER 21: HENNA ASHRAF

Henna is a software engineer and has been working in IT sector for last 22 years. She lives in London with her husband and two children. Earlier this year, she started thinking that she can't solely depend on her salary and needs to have multiple income streams and that's what led her to the world of online arbitrage.

How has a failure or apparent failure, set you up for later success? Do you have a "favourite failure" of yours?

My favourite one is my driving test. I failed it 6 times. I used to be disappointed every time I failed but I was firm that I will not give up. Every time, I reviewed why I failed and tried to work on my weak areas. On 7th attempt, when I passed my practical driving test, I was over the moon.

What is one of the best or most worthwhile investments you've ever made? (Could be time, money, energy etc.)

Migrating to UK to give my family and me more opportunities and a better future. This was not easy as coming from a developing country (Pakistan), there were lots of challenges and sacrifices but if I look back, that was the best decision.

In the last 5 years, what new belief, behaviour, or habit has most improved your life?

'The only person who is a blocker to your success is you'. I was used to come up with many excuses for not doing certain things but in last few years, I realised that I can't control situations but I do have control on how I react to a situation and since then, my perspective of life changed for good.

What best advice would you give to someone about to enter the world of arbitrage?

I believe it's very important to enjoy what you do. If you think, arbitrage business model is something, which you can do for long term, then do not pay attention to the problems other people are facing. Take the plunge and go with the flow. Problems will be there but you will also get the solutions and that's what will make you successful.

What are bad recommendations you hear relating to arbitrage?

I don't think there is any bad recommendation. Something, which works for me, may not work for someone else as everyone's work style and priorities are different.

When you feel overwhelmed or unfocused, or have lost your focus temporarily what do you do?

Since last few years, whenever I face an issue, I write that and then once that issue is resolved, I write that too in front of that. So, whenever I feel unfocused or overwhelmed, I go through that list and tell myself that if I could overcome those problems, I can overcome the current issue too.

Another thing, what I do is breaking a bigger task into smaller ones. This way, I found to complete the tasks easily and feel a sense of achievement. I use Google Keep to track all my tasks and feel accomplished when I mark them as done.

Business Models: Online Arbitrage.

TRIBE MEMBER 22: MARTYNAS VALKUNAS

Martynas is an IT professional working and living in London looking for alternatives to generate   income.

How has a failure or apparent failure, set you up for later success? Do you have a "favourite failure" of yours?

Of course. I noticed that through the hardest and most difficult times, I have achieved the most. It feels like my brain switches on to look for opportunities when I cannot back down. I believe that everything happens for the reason. One step at the time. It is not a failure if you keep standing up.

What is one of the best or most worthwhile investments you've ever made? (Could be time, money, energy etc.)

The best investment is you. Once you learn something, it will stay with you forever.

In the last 5 years, what new belief, behaviour, or habit has most improved your life?

All the great things take time. Be patient, be consistent and one step at the time.

What best advice would you give to someone about to enter the world of arbitrage?

Just start doing it. The hardest part is to start.

What are bad recommendations you hear relating to arbitrage?

None so far as I am few months old in this area.

When you feel overwhelmed or unfocused, or have lost your focus temporarily what do you do?

Take a step back, do what i like as part of my hobbies. But I always search for the balance to keep the focus on all the time. It is not about the destination, it is about the journey.

TRIBE MEMBER 23: EMMA HAMILTON

Emma is an Ecommerce Business Owner and Business Coach specialising in the Amazon Marketplace. Started Amazon FBA in 2017 after stumbling across some videos on YouTube...started working on her online business whilst working fulltime as a Media, Communications and PR Lead. Whilst at her previous job, she was 'minding my own business' a term she learnt from the book Rich Dad, Poor Day.

As an entrepreneur, she believes multiple streams of income are important, hence, branching out into coaching and other online revenue streams. Have helped tens of people get started with Amazon FBA through 1-1 personalised coaching and helped hundreds of others get motivated and take that leap into starting their online business.

How has a failure or apparent failure, set you up for later success? Do you have a "favourite failure" of yours?

Back in 2011, I had a YouTube Channel that was doing very well and often my videos were in the top trending videos section, most discussed etc., however, I just stopped because 'I didn't feel like it' - it taught me a very important lesson, in life we go through ups and downs...but continuous persistent action is imperative to success. This has taught me, when the going gets tough...push through those barriers...this helps to build resilience. Additionally, it taught me the importance of having goals and a definite purpose in life, so you know where you are going in life rather than wondering through aimlessly, so when the going does get tough you can revert to your goals and helps to guide me back on the right path.

What is one of the best or most worthwhile investments you've ever made? (Could be time, money, energy etc.)

Books - it enables me to leverage the experience of others. The successes I have had over the last few years I attribute firmly to my journey of self-development, which simply started with picking up a book. One of my favourite books of all time is Think and Grow Rich by Napoleon Hill - it helped me build the desire for what I really wanted, which in turn helped me to become laser focused.

It is very easy in this day and age to get shiny object syndrome and jump from one thing to another without giving something chance to come into full fruition. I implement the strategies within this book daily which include reading the self-confidence formula.

In the last 5 years, what new belief, behaviour, or habit has most improved your life?

Habit - my morning ritual. I implemented this habit after reading the Miracle Morning, which was gifted, to me by a good friend of mine. Before, I used to be very flexible with how I started the day...I am lazy by nature so it wasn't uncommon for me to stay up until 3am and wake at 12pm - would feel very groggy and unproductive. Implementing a morning ritual has transformed my life, I wake up with more energy and focus.

My morning ritual consists of the Life SAVERS

S. Silence
A. Affirmations
V. Visualisations
E. Exercise
R. Reading
S. Scribbling/Journaling

What best advice would you give to someone about to enter the world of arbitrage?

First, identify your goal and establish your 'why', what would you like to achieve as this differs with everyone. Then, identify a strategy that matches your starting investment. It's very easy to get carried away buying tools and services - however; I would say invest in those as your business grows.

Do plenty of research or invest in a course or a coach, a good course/coach can save you hundreds if not thousands. Additionally persistence, dedicate yourself to the process and seek out groups online for support.

What are bad recommendations you hear relating to arbitrage?

Recommendations surrounding deal analysis, I hear advice that you can rely on best sellers rank alone, however, the best sellers rank gives a snapshot into the selling history but not the full history. I recommend investing in a tool like Keepa as you can thoroughly analyse deals.... see how long they have been selling over a period of time, not just the last hour. Analysing deals thoroughly prior to purchasing is essential.

When you feel overwhelmed or unfocused, or have lost your focus temporarily what do you do?

I'd be kind to myself. It is easy to get frustrated when you feel unfocused...however, when these times do occur, I will treat myself to a massage or meal with friends or a family member and then I continue with the goals I have set myself.

In times when I felt unfocused, instead of stopping, I have continued and looked back and felt proud of the work I have achieved. When I feel overwhelmed, I write down what needs to be done and prioritise them in order of importance. Rome wasn't build in a day and I have realised things in life take time, it is not about the destination but more about the journey. Also speaking with other family members, friends, other entrepreneur helps - it is something a lot of people face and speaking with others can help keep you motivated and stay on track.

Facebook: https://www.facebook.com/groups/theamazondream

YouTube: https://www.youtube.com/emmalouisehamilton

Business Models: Online Arbitrage.

GETTING STARTED WITH ONLINE ARBITRAGE

Now that you have learned from some of the best operating sellers online, it's about taking massive action on anything you learned. I wanted to include a recent video playlist that I created that could allow you learn everything from starting to make your first sales. This is a great free course that will share a lot with you.

Watching this video, you will learn everything you need to make your first sales giving you an overview of the business and what is achievable.

Video Link: https://youtu.be/hGgLZA6q2T8

Watching this video, you will learn everything you need to start building your sourcing machine that will work for you everyday on autopilot.

Video Link: https://youtu.be/7-LspVeo4OM

Watching this video, you will learn everything you need about taking advantage of a number of money hacks that will give you compounded profits in your business.

Video Link: https://youtu.be/50cZcu0kf3c

Watching this video, you will learn everything you need to begin shipping to Amazon's fulfilment centers accurately and at speed.

Video Link: https://youtu.be/kuL_OcJEKdQ

PRODUCTIVITY TIPS FOR AMAZON SELLERS

When it comes to building the business, a huge part of this is organisation and productivity. I call this taking massive action! I wanted to include a number of what I believe is the best insightful videos I have around taking massive action. Enjoy.

Watching this video, you will learn 23 amazing tips about setting up your massive action eco-system. Everything will promote action and productivity in your life.

Video Link: https://youtu.be/PkYRB8E-PSM

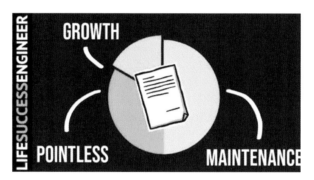

Watching this video, you will learn what I call "Growth Vs Maintenance Vs Pointless". This is fundamental building block to taking action in the right areas everyday.

Video Link: https://youtu.be/nr0yCRxiQjl

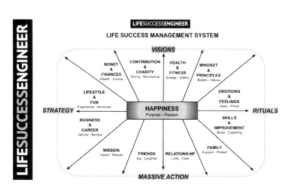

Watching this video, you will learn about the Life Success Management System that can introduce organisation in life.

Video Link: https://youtu.be/Tw9sikHZ8Bc

RESOURCES & RECOMMENDATIONS

Over the last few of years, I have used products and services that have helped me Improve in all areas of my life.

I have explored and invested in many things from online training programs, mentors, books, seminars, and everything in between. I get asked all the time, which are the best resources I would recommend so I wanted to create this page that personally shares with you what has impacted my life in a positive way. Everything on this page I have had experience with and I love it to the point where I will confidently recommend it to you.

I did not want to hold back so you will find everything on this page from Online Business to Personal Development resources that could suit you and be exactly what you have been looking for.

https://www.lifesuccessengineer.com/resources

Master Level Sourcing Strategies (Multiple Streams Of Sourcing Products)

Online Arbitrage

Level 1 – Manually Sourcing
Level 2 - Sourcing List - Video Demo: https://youtu.be/rITu1IS4i6k
Level 3 - Virtual Assistant Training - Video Demo: https://youtu.be/wwDtXNvDNqU
Level 4 - Automated Sourcing
Level 5 - Resource Pooling

Wholesale

Attend Tradeshow - Video Demo: https://youtu.be/Rl6sUX1Elqs

Organisation Via Master sheets

Start using Mastersheets In Your Business.
Video Demo:
https://www.youtube.com/playlist?list=PLPXwW5tVvu8F93Glxp0vXm1PUmBmJLFzb

Preparation & Shipping To Amazon's Fulfilment Centres

Use A Prep Service:
http://fbaprepserviceuk.com/

Use The FREE Prep Guide:
http://fbaprepserviceuk.com/getstarted

Time Saving Senior Virtual Assistants

Hire a senior assistant that will save lots of time.
https://onlinearbitrageservices.com/collections/assistants

Video Demo: https://youtu.be/1I2ZH1eKiSw

Business Management

Integrate Asana into your business for task management of your team:
https://asana.com/

Introduce Management weekly reports. Please view the following videos:

Virtual Team:
https://youtu.be/xrJ6lINQ-P8

Warehouse:
https://youtu.be/g0IG41QcVuo

Inventory Health

Create Inventory Health Systems for:

- Products older than 6 weeks.
- Products not sold in last month.
- Products at Min in Repricer.
- Automation in Repricer.

30 Day Trial With Repricer Express:
https://www.onlinearbitragemastery.com/repricerexpress

Inventory Replenishing

How accurate are your purchasing numbers? Take a sample.
How many repeat products you getting every month?

Financial Management

Use Seller Board (2 Months Free)
https://www.onlinearbitragemastery.com/sellerboard

Best Credit Card (40,000 Free Points)
http://lifesuccessengineer.com/amex

Education & Coaching

Enrol into Online Arbitrage Mastery for 3 day trial:
https://lifesuccessengineer.mykajabi.com/online-arbitrage-mastery-2019-enrolment

Coaching Sessions
https://www.lifesuccessengineer.com/coaching

Mastermind & Support

Join us on Facebook to hang out with other like minded people:
http://lifesuccessengineer.com/fbgroup

Events & Masterminds

Come to the next event and hang out with others:
http://lifesuccessengineer.com/events

Success Interviews:

Jake Diego - $60,000+ In 30 Days.
https://youtu.be/xuw5Rvf3MJA

Adam Kupinski - £45,000+ In 30 Days.
https://youtu.be/9soM1GevAnQ

CONCLUSION

Hopefully by now you are super excited and you are ready to start immediately taking massive action!

I want to take this moment again to thank all the amazing people that have contributed to the creation of this book. It really is a gift from Amazon Sellers to Amazon Sellers.

Please feel free to reach out to any of the people featured in the book and share with them how great the answers were?

If you don't mind, it would be great for you to support the book by leaving a review on Amazon Kindle. By giving this a review, it will allow the book to reach more people and support more people. You can do this simply by heading to Amazon and clicking on leave a review.

And that is it, the Tribe Of Arbitragers Edition 1 is now complete! I hope this has been everything you hoped it would be. I'm really looking forward to the next wave of members joining the Tribe!

This is Kev here from Life Success Engineer, inspiring you everyday to keep taking massive action!

To your massive success,

Kev "Massive Action" Blackburn

LIFESUCCESSENGINEER

Life Success Engineer:
https://www.lifesuccessengineer.com/

Massive Action Academy:
https://www.lifesuccessengineer.com/academy

YouTube Channel: http://lifesuccessengineer.com/youtube

Instagram Page: http://lifesuccessengineer.com/instagram

Printed in Great Britain
by Amazon